MW01234569

FOOTSTEPS TO
AmericA

Dominican Americans

Dominican Americans

by Alexandra Bandon

New Discovery Books
Parsippany, New Jersey

ACKNOWLEDGMENT

Special thanks to the immigrants who shared their personal stories. Their names have been changed to protect their privacy.

PHOTO CREDITS

Front cover: Mary Ellen Matthews; Front and back cover (flag photo): Richard Bachmann
The Bettmann Archive: 9
Mary Ellen Matthews: 10, 36, 39, 51, 54, 67, 76, 79, 82, 85, 87, 93, 95
AP/Wide World Photos: 18, 24, 30, 34, 45, 104
UPI/Bettmann: 21
Reuters Bettmann: 74

Published by New Discovery Books, an imprint of Silver Burdett Press.
A Simon & Schuster Company
299 Jefferson Road, Parsippany, NJ 07054

Printed in the United States of America
10 9 8 7 6 5 4 3 2 1

LIBRARY OF CONGRESS CATALOGING–IN–PUBLICATION DATA
Bandon, Alexandra.
Dominican Americans / by Alexandra Bandon. — 1st ed.
p.   cm. — (Footsteps to America)
Includes bibliographical references (p.   ) and index.
ISBN 0-02-768152-1
1. Dominican Americans—Juvenile literature. [1. Dominican Americans.]
I. Title. II. Series.
E184.D6B36   1995
304.8'7293073—dc20   94-36289

Contents

Part I

The Land They Left Behind

≡ 1 ≡

Why Do They Leave?

The Island of Hispaniola

South of Florida, between the islands of Cuba and Puerto Rico, lies a large island called Hispaniola. Two countries share Hispaniola: Haiti, the smaller country on the west and the Dominican Republic on the east. Haiti has been much in the news in the 1980s and 1990s because of the many thousands of its people seeking refuge in the United States from political and economic hardships. However, of the two countries, it is the Dominican Republic from which more immigrants have come to the United States, numbering steadily in the tens of thousands each year since the 1960s. Yet little attention has been paid to this quiet immigration.

The Dominican Republic occupies the eastern two-thirds of Hispaniola. To the north lies the Atlantic Ocean; to the south, the Caribbean Sea. Hispaniola was one of Columbus's first stops in the New World in 1492 (actually, the *Santa Maria* ran aground there). That year, on the northern shore, Columbus established the first Spanish settlement in the Western Hemisphere. Santo Domingo, founded on the southern coast in 1496, is the oldest permanent settlement in the New World. Because of Columbus's glowing descriptions back in Spain about the beautiful island he had discovered, Hispaniola is often referred to as "the land Columbus loved."

This illustration shows Columbus landing on Hispaniola in 1492. The Dominican Republic is the site of the oldest Spanish settlement in the New World.

Across the 80-mile Mona Passage to the east of Hispaniola is Puerto Rico, the part of the United States nearest to the Dominican Republic. Puerto Rico is the first destination of many Dominican emigrants (people who leave their country to settle permanently in another country are emigrants; those who enter and settle in another country are immigrants). Dominicans have been coming to the United States in small numbers for most of the twentieth century. The Dominican Republic's history with the United States dates back to 1916, when President Woodrow Wilson sent United States Marines to invade the island and quell the political turmoil that had raged there for decades.

The Marines' presence, from 1916 to 1924, left a lasting political and cultural impression on the small country. Since then, Dominicans have made the United States and the United States territory of Puerto Rico their prime destinations when emigrating. Once a

Dominican immigrants have migrated to the United States by the tens of thousands since the 1960s.

Dominican decides to stay in the United States permanently, he or she becomes a Dominican American, and his or her United States-born children are second-generation Dominican Americans. Dominican Americans are considered to be Hispanics or Latinos. Either term includes Spanish-speaking Americans, whether of Mexican, Puerto Rican, South American, or Central American origin.

Trujillo's Regime

After the withdrawal of the Marines in 1924, the Dominican Republic's political situation stabilized but not without some sacrifice of human rights. In 1930, Rafael Leonidas Trujillo Molina, a lieutenant in the U.S. Marines-trained Dominican army, overthrew the president of the Dominican Republic. He won the office in an election that year. Trujillo then declared himself Generalissimo, a title that allowed him to maintain harsh military and political control of the country.

In the midst of a worldwide economic depression, Trujillo instituted an economic policy that increased government control over agriculture and industry as well as strengthened economic ties with the United States. But he demanded major sacrifices from the people of the Dominican Republic. He suspended democratic elections, stifled unionization, and exacted high taxes from Dominicans to pay for government projects. Anyone who disagreed with his politics was in danger of being subjected to arrest, torture, or death. Trujillo's policies brought peace, stability, and economic prosperity to the Dominican Republic but at a cost of freedom and human lives. To this day, his regime is both denounced

continued on page 17

Cahonabo Pérez
No More Fear

Cahonabo Pérez is 63 years old. He owns two grocery and general-item stores in the Washington Heights section of New York City, where he also lives.

I came to New York in 1958. It was not so easy to do back then, but I was desperate. This was when Trujillo was the dictator in the Dominican Republic. I was young and maybe foolish and spoke out about his abuses of power. One day a friend and I were taken from the street. I was beaten and questioned and released. Who knows why I am still alive. I never saw my friend again. These days such people are called the "disappeared ones." So, you see, it still goes on. I get tired sometimes thinking how nothing changes.

Anyway, I was fearful for my life. I couldn't emigrate because that devil, Trujillo, didn't allow it. I managed to cross the Mona Passage, 80 miles of bad sea to Puerto Rico. Not that I was welcomed with open arms there, either, but at least I spoke the language and was not in constant fear for my life. I quickly made friends in Puerto Rico and obtained illegal documents. I didn't wish to stay there because it was too difficult to find good work. So, as a Puerto Rican, I came "legally" to the United States.

It's okay. I can talk about it now, because during the declared amnesty in 1986, I finally became a truthful man and am now a legal immigrant. It's a worry I'm glad to be done with.

I wish I could say that everything was fine once I came to New York, but it wasn't. Some of it was because I was so angry at the United States for supporting Trujillo. Some of it was because most of the people in Washington Heights back then were Puerto Ricans and they did not exactly welcome us Dominicans with open arms. Some of it was because it took me a while to speak English. But I made it! My first job was as a waiter in a Puerto Rican restaurant. This was a lucky break because the owner of that restaurant also owned a store where I went to work later with an agreement to buy him out. He was a good man, and because of him I am doing well to this day.

My wife came here in 1965 with her parents. We married soon after meeting. I think her parents were a little unhappy with me at first—being older and not quite legal, but that soon passed. We had three sons and a good but too-short life together. She died in 1990 of cancer. Yolanda. You won't meet a finer woman. My boys and I are doing fine. I'm a grandpa now. How quickly time goes. One day I was a struggling young man and now I'm a grandpa. I look around me and the Puerto Rican community I moved into is now almost all Dominican Americans. Isn't that something? I never dreamed I would live again in a community of my own people. I like it. Not so much prejudice about color this way or where you are from or why you are here. Just less questions to answer.

My oldest boy runs the stores with me. The other two work part time at the stores, but both are in college. That was Yolanda's doing. She was very big on education. Still her influence lives on. The boys are very American in some ways, espe-

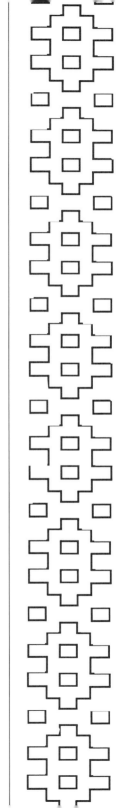

cially the youngest. They all wish to stay in America but maybe not New York. I plan to go back to the Dominican Republic. They laugh and say, "Right, dad." But I mean it. I will buy a little house in the country and count the bananas on the trees! Okay, who knows, but I haven't given up the dream.

There is an even older man than me who lives nearby. He plants corn in a center divider on Broadway. Yes, it's true. They even wrote about him in the paper. He has a real garden in the middle of the street. It's a beautiful thing to see. I finally met him. He said he planted the corn to remind himself of home. Now he comes to the store sometimes, and we have coffee and talk about home and the old farms and how being boys in the country was such a fine thing. This has given me back good memories of my country, which is why I think of returning.

The boys are probably right, though. I have my family here and my grandson. Maybe after all these years I should just call this home. I guess it is. My boys say, "Dad, you're a legal man now, speak out." So maybe I will take up politics in my old age. I came to this country for freedom. Maybe now is the time to practice it.

for its harsh measures and highly admired for its success in bringing order to a volatile situation.

Trujillo was assassinated in 1961. Prior to his death, emigration from the Dominican Republic had been severely restricted.
Trujillo feared emigrants might cause him political problems by
spreading the word about his oppressive policies, so only a small
number of Dominicans emigrated to the United States before the
early 1960s. It wasn't until after Trujillo died that great numbers
of Dominicans began to arrive in this country.

Political Turmoil

After Trujillo's assassination, the political situation in the
Dominican Republic went through numerous changes. At first,
there was little unrest because Trujillo had ruled with a figurehead
president, Joaquín Balaguer, who continued Trujillo's policies. In
addition, the military maintained tight control over the people,
often detaining those they thought may have been associated with
the assassination and sometimes executing them on the spot.

Balaguer couldn't maintain control, however, and in the
beginning of 1962, he was overthrown by a military coup d'état.
Balaguer was taken from office and sent into exile by army rebels
who feared losing power. But just two weeks later, the rebels
themselves were overthrown by factions favoring a democracy, and
the first democratic elections since Trujillo came into power were
planned for December 1962. Balaguer remained in exile.

In the 1962 elections Juan Bosch, a member of the
Dominican Revolutionary Party (PRD), was elected president.

Bosch worked quickly to repair the economy, which had begun to falter in the last decade of Trujillo's regime. He also tried to move the Dominican Republic rapidly toward democracy, instead of keeping the military-supported dictatorship that Trujillo had maintained. But in September of 1963, just seven months after Bosch's inauguration, the military staged another coup d'état and Bosch was sent into exile.

The military set up a government run by a three-man committee. But this civilian committee was just a front for a corrupt, repressive military. At this point, the situation in the Dominican Republic was so unstable that many Dominicans tried to leave the country and escape the confusion. The military was desperately trying to hold on to power, but that meant many civilians were in danger of abuse by soldiers.

Meanwhile, the PRD and Bosch planned a countercoup, and other political factions plotted their own seizure of power. In April of 1965, the PRD started a revolution and moved to reinstate Bosch as president. But this time, the United States was worried that true power would fall into the hands of Communists associated with Cuba. President Lyndon B. Johnson ordered that American troops move to support the military government against Bosch and the leftists. Under the guise of protecting American citizens living in the Dominican Republic, 23,000 United States troops invaded the Dominican Republic. The threat of the Dominican Republic turning into "another Cuba," as the United States government put it, was insignificant. But at the height of the Cold War, the mere threat of Communist forces in power in the Western Hemisphere sent the United States into battle.

Eventually, the United States presence brought order to the

chaotic political situation, and in 1966, Joaquín Balaguer was reelected. With Balaguer, the Dominican dictatorship was restored.

The Country Under Balaguer

Balaguer ruled the Dominican Republic from 1966 to 1978, a period marked by general economic prosperity for the country. Under Balaguer, tourism in the balmy Caribbean country flourished; foreign investment, which boosted the production rates of the country, increased; and the price of sugar, the main export of the Dominican Republic, rose dramatically. The country appeared to be in good shape thanks to Balaguer's reforms and government projects. Many of the changes were supported by United States aid.

But only the wealthiest benefited from the progress made under Balaguer. Though the average income in the country rose during his regime, it was because the rich became richer. The standard of living of the poor actually fell. Unemployment was between 30 and 40 percent. That meant that two out of every five people in the Dominican Republic had no work. Illiteracy was widespread, poverty was rampant, people were ill-fed, and many children died at a young age.

Most of the people leaving the Dominican Republic in the late 1960s and early 1970s were the poor. Living as squatters in abandoned houses or in makeshift shanties near the cities, they had no modern conveniences, no jobs, no medical care, and no help from the government. Their only hope was to look for work elsewhere.

By 1978, most of the good fortune for the Dominican

In 1965, American troops tried to quell a volatile political situation in the Dominican Republic and establish a democratic, non-communist government. They were met with some resistance from the Dominican people.

Republic had ended. The world market for sugar had slowed, inflation was high, and the necessities, such as food and fuel, generally cost more. Additionally, Dominicans were becoming discouraged with Balaguer's corruption and with the government's constant terrorist attacks against the popularly supported PRD.

Elections held in 1978 put the PRD candidate, Antonio Guzmán, in the president's office. Balaguer tried to seize the ballot boxes when it became clear that Guzmán was going to win, but President Jimmy Carter warned him that the United States would take action if Balaguer interfered with the election. Once in office, Guzmán moved immediately to lift some of the oppression of Balaguer's reign, granting more political freedom and supporting human rights.

Human Rights Violations

One of the reasons Guzmán and the PRD won the presidency was their promise to end the bullying that characterized the Trujillo and Balaguer regimes. But by 1986, widespread reports of human rights abuses were accusing the PRD government (now under Salvador Jorge Blanco, elected in 1982) of repeating the cycle of arrests and torture.

Some pointed the finger of blame at the police. The accusers said that people were unjustly detained, arrested, and tortured, not because of criminal acts or political dissent, but because they had fallen into police disfavor. Those people had joined the *desaparacidos,* or the "disappeared ones." In 1985 alone, the Dominican Commission for Human Rights documented 65 *desaparacidos.*

Others blamed the human rights violations and corruption on Blanco's government. They said the government was afraid to investigate the illegal acts of the police. The PRD, the party that had once pushed for freedom under the dictatorship of Trujillo and the presidency of Balaguer, was itself now accused of illegal detentions, beatings, and deaths of Dominicans.

Unfortunately, reports of human rights violations didn't end with Jorge Blanco's government. Throughout the 1980s and into the 1990s, the government of the Dominican Republic has continued to be accused of illegal arrests, detentions, and beatings. In addition, some Dominicans keep extra cash handy for bribes to corrupt government officials and police.

The victims of some of the worst abuse have been Haitians

who have migrated from their own country in search of work in the sugar cane fields. Haitians are seen by Dominicans as a threat to jobs and the economy. Anyone thought to be Haitian is in danger of being beaten, not only by the Dominican police but by any Dominican who has a strong prejudice against the Haitians.

The Economic Decline of the 1980s

Under the succession of PRD presidents from Guzmán to Blanco, the government of the Dominican Republic tried to fix the Dominican economy in the early 1980s by controlling prices. In order to do that, the government had to subsidize farmers and food imports. That is, it had to pay farmers and the importers so that they could afford to keep down the prices of such basics as rice, beans, cornmeal, bananas, and sugar. But the cost of producing these goods was continuing to grow, while the buying power of the Dominican currency was dropping.

The Dominican government owned a lot of the manufacturing sector, including land confiscated from Trujillo's estate after his assassination and numerous sugar refineries bought to keep them from closing down. After Trujillo died, the government nationalized (took as government property) many industries—including cement, glass, vegetable oil, shoes, tobacco, chocolate, and more. But these government-owned factories were competing with private manufacturers and were operating at a loss. The plants were mismanaged and had maintenance problems. They were overstaffed and generally inoperative, and a lack of government action

held back the entire manufacturing sector. For every cent these industries lost in operation, the government lost money subsidizing them.

In addition, the state of the poor had not improved. Half a million Dominicans—out of a population of 7 million—either did not own enough land on which to grow food to feed their families or did not own land at all. Forty percent of the population was illiterate. Three out of every four children were undernourished and diseased; 10 percent died before the age of five. The monthly minimum wage of a Dominican worker in the early 1980s wasn't enough to support one person, let alone a whole family.

The Dominican economy was in great trouble. It owed money to many other countries in the world, but it couldn't afford to pay its debts. By 1984, the International Monetary Fund (IMF), an

Joaquín Balaguer after his election to the Dominican presidency in 1986. Balaguer has been accused of crippling the Dominican economy by covering his excessive spending with the printing of more money.

agency of the United Nations that works to stabilize international economies, was called in to get the country to pay its creditors. The Dominican Republic hoped to receive a $430 million loan from the IMF, but the Fund required that the country institute austerity measures first. Austerity measures are government-controlled changes that are meant to bring the country's economy to the level of economics of other countries.

For the Dominican Republic, this meant discontinuing the food subsidies, cutting public spending, and devaluing the currency. Overnight, the price of food, transportation, and medicine tripled. The people in the lower class struggled as their earning power was cut in half. By April of 1984, there were widespread demonstrations to protest the price hikes.

Citizens clashed with police and troops. Demonstrators threw rocks at the stores accused of price gouging, then looted the stores and rioted. The troops sent by President Blanco fired into the crowd and shot suspected looters on the spot. In total, 100 people died, 400 were injured, and 4,000 were arrested. Fearing a true revolution, President Blanco refused to put into effect any more austerity measures.

In 1985, Blanco was faced with even more demonstrations, this time by people in the rural areas. Four rural leaders were killed when protestors demonstrated against Blanco's failure to keep an election promise to give land to 8,000 peasant families each year of his presidential term. It was predicted that year that Blanco would lose the next election to Balaguer.

He did, and Joaquín Balaguer was in power yet again. But he was faced with an ever deteriorating Dominican economy. In 1986, President Ronald Reagan cut back on the amount of sugar the

United States was allowed to import from the Dominican Republic,
a move continued in 1989 by his successor, George Bush. By 1989
the amount of sugar exported to the Dominican Republic's largest
sugar customer had dropped to one eighth of its volume in 1979.
The Dominican sugar industry was forced to close down several
plantations and processing plants, which, of course, led to layoffs
of thousands of agricultural workers.

Balaguer's response to the failing economy was to begin
many new government building projects to boost employment—
and to pay for the projects by printing more money. But printing
extra money only means that the money can't buy as much. So
inflation in the Dominican Republic in the late 1980s was sky
high. By 1990 it had reached 100 percent, up from 59 percent in
1989 and a mere 6 percent in 1986.

Because Dominican money then couldn't buy as much, more
Dominican people qualified as "poor." In 1986, *one fourth* of
Dominicans were living below the poverty line, a standard set by
the government to identify earnings below which people were offi-
cially considered to be poor. By 1990, *half* of all Dominicans were
living in poverty. However, Balaguer preferred to keep printing
money. This allowed him to avoid imposing any more austerity
measures, which he feared would spark another uprising.

In the meantime, the quality of living for all Dominicans dis-
integrated. Rising fuel costs caused an energy shortage. Entire
sections of Santo Domingo, the capital, were blacked out for hours
at a time because the power companies had to conserve fuel.
Gasoline for cars was scarce and therefore expensive. Running
water was even more scarce, available as little as one hour each
day. The wealthy survived by paying outrageous prices for diesel

April 24, 1984, Santo Domingo. Riots protesting rising costs due to austerity measures left 100 dead and 400 injured. Here, a youth is held at gunpoint.

fuel for their private generators. The poor just went without. Only half the population ate adequately and had safe drinking water. The average life expectancy in the Dominican Republic was 62 years, more than ten years below that in the United States.

In 1990, just before the inauguration for his sixth term and after an election in which he defeated Juan Bosch, Balaguer was forced to institute additional austerity measures. Balaguer had resisted making an agreement with the IMF, even though it would have brought in much-needed American dollars, because he feared losing some of his power. In the end, he devalued the currency and doubled the prices of basic goods. Unfortunately, the miserable quality of living pushed Dominicans to protest. In June of 1990, the major trade unions called a general strike. Violent demonstrations followed, in which 14 people died and hundreds were wounded during clashes with police.

Columbus's Lighthouse

The 1990s proved better for the Dominican economy. Even though fuel shortages worsened during the 1991 Gulf War and blackouts persisted, the inflation rate fell from 1990's 100 percent high to 4 percent in 1991. In 1993, inflation had dropped to 2 percent. Industrial production, which had plummeted in the late 1980s, rose again in the early 1990s. And the Dominican Republic began once again to make payments to its creditors.

Most of this new prosperity, however, never reached the poor and the middle-class Dominicans. Many were still stuck below the poverty line, with one out of four unemployed. A pair of

continued on page 31

Francisca Linares
Working Toward the Future

Francisca Linares is 27 years old, married, and works in a sewing factory in New Jersey. She lives in the Washington Heights section of New York City.

I have lived here since I was 19 years old. My husband came first because he had a brother in New York who was legal. I joined him after our first child was born. So our first was born in Santo Domingo and our second in New York City. It has not been easy here, but it is still better than what we had in the Dominican Republic.

No, I don't really want to talk about those days. To tell the truth, they are best forgotten. If it were not for my parents, I would try to wipe my memory clean. I thank God every day that I am at least able to send them a little money every month to make their life better. My husband, Miguel, and I do not wish to return.

Besides, I sometimes think everyone from there is here now. Look where I live. We are all Dominican Americans! I meet people sometimes in the store that I knew as a child. It is different that way than I thought it would be—how would you say, finding the past here. I can buy the same things, eat the same food, speak my language. You can hear that I try very hard to speak English right, but it is still a big struggle.

My husband works as a janitor. He cleans many office buildings in Manhattan and is paid very well. After my children were old enough for school, I began to work, too. I take a bus to New Jersey and work as a seamstress in a shirt factory. It is owned by people from the Dominican Republic. They don't pay so well, but I can't really do anything but sew. And I like the women I work with.

The days are sometimes too long, though. I am very tired when I get home, and then we still have dinner to cook and children to bathe and things to discuss. Miguel is good to help me. I don't think back home he would do these things, but here it is different. I like it because this way the children know him better and I get more rest.

I say I want to wipe the Dominican Republic from my mind, but in reality I do miss it sometimes. Especially at work while I am sewing. The thing I like to think about is when I learned to sew. I was able to go to school until I was eight or nine. The nuns taught us how to embroider. When we wanted to do something special for them, we would embroider little handkerchiefs with hair from our head. I know, it seems funny now. But it was beautiful at the time to pull a long hair from your own head and make it into a beautiful design. It is so different now in the factory: nothing personal or beautiful, just sleeves onto shirts, collars onto blouses.

Where my kids go to school there are no nuns and no embroidery, but they will get to go to the end. We will make sure that they graduate. And it is all for free. Sometimes I think this is the best thing about America, better than the money.

Here where we live there is also an organization called the Alianza Dominicana. It has been much help to me. It is where I learned English when the babies were small. The organization helped me to learn about the schools and the different ways in America. There are problems here with drugs, and I want to make sure my children don't get around that type of person. The people at the Alianza teach us how to teach our children. It is very good because I want very much for my little ones.

So we work and get tired and try to do the right thing, just like most people. I guess that makes us not too different from other Americans, don't you think?

* * *

shoes still cost a month's salary, and food was expensive com-
pared with the wages Dominicans could earn. Again, only the rich
became richer.

During this period of economic growth, Balaguer began a pet
project that he had been planning for several years and that would
greatly affect the poorest residents of Santo Domingo. October
1992 marked the 500th anniversary, or quincentennial, of
Columbus's landing in the New World. Since the Dominican
Republic was "the land Columbus loved," Balaguer hoped to boost
tourism by building a giant lighthouse in honor of the explorer. An
800-foot-long and 150-foot-tall cross-shaped building, its light
would shine so brightly it could be seen as far away as Puerto
Rico. Both Pope John Paul II and King Juan Carlos of Spain were
invited to attend the dedication ceremony.

The problem was that adjacent to the site of the lighthouse
lay the Santo Domingo slum known as Maquiteria, filled with
squatters and shanties. Balaguer proposed to pave over the slum,
which he considered an eyesore and an obstacle to tourism, and
then to build new housing in the suburbs for its residents. But
even before the houses were torn down, he ordered that a large
wall be built to hide the area from visitors. The residents called it
"the wall of shame and hypocrisy" and pointed out that it turned
the streets into dead ends. Behind the wall, there were no government services, no electricity or running water in the schools, and
the unpaved streets were covered with garbage. Electricity for the
area was supplied by makeshift wiring that the residents connected to the power lines.

Eventually, the area was cleared. Under military supervision,
bulldozers rolled into the shantytown and flattened the houses,

which were made from wood, tin, or cardboard. But residents were given no relief or compensation for their lost homes. They were told they'd be rehoused, but some residents still had no new housing three years after being evicted. They simply became homeless, though government supporters were given the new, modern apartments. In addition, the bright lights of the monument required enormous power. But with the power shortages, turning on the lighthouse meant blacking out the adjacent barrio.

In the end, Balaguer spent several hundred million dollars on this one project. It was touted as an event of great celebration, with the Pope expected to inaugurate the monument. But Pope John Paul II, who was visiting the Dominican Republic at the time, and King Juan Carlos both refused to attend the dedication because of the controversies over Columbus's hero status.

This million-dollar lighthouse was built in Santo Domingo to commemorate the quincentennial of Columbus's landing on Hispaniola. The inset photo shows the nearby slum, hidden by the ten-foot "wall of shame."

Columbus is now considered by some to have brought geno-cide and violent oppression to the native residents of the New World. In fact, of the 8 million Taino Arawak Indians living on Hispaniola when Columbus landed, all had died of disease or over-work as slaves within 50 years of his arrival. Dominicans, none of whom have any Taino heritage, see the cruelty in the Spanish con-quest but feel it was justified as necessary and unavoidable in civi-lizing and Christianizing the natives. Dominicans unconditionally praise Columbus as a hero. However, the pomp and grandeur of the monument dedication was dampened by the controversy sur-rounding Columbus's ventures. Even President Balaguer missed the dedication ceremony because of a death in his family.

The Emigration Solution

For the Dominicans who were most affected by the degener-ating conditions, the only solution was emigration. The govern-ment agreed. Emigration alleviated many of the government's responsibilities for services and for social programs. Water, trans-portation, housing, health care, education, and social security were all inadequate, and emigration lifted some of the burden on the government.

In addition, emigration has become the second largest source of revenues for the Dominican Republic. When Dominicans leave their country, they usually send back to their families part of their earnings from their new locations. Dominican expatriates in the United States send back between $600 million and $800 million a year to their relatives in the Dominican Republic, who then spend the money on consumer goods, thus supporting the Dominican economy. Entire towns are supported by the money that comes from Dominican Americans who have chosen to move from one of the poorest countries in the Western Hemisphere to the wealthiest. Without the money sent by Dominican Americans, the Dominican economy would collapse completely.

Why the United States?

The Lure of the Dollar

Wh
hen the Dominican Republic needed help with its economy, it naturally looked to the United States government for a loan. In fact, when the first austerity measures were instituted in 1984, the United States was expecting to collect loan payments as one of the Dominican Republic's biggest creditors. The American dollar has become an integral part of the Dominican economy, so it is no surprise that Dominicans would go straight to the source when looking for a new life outside their country.

The average Dominicans make about $10 a week laboring in industries that require a lot of work. In the United States, workers earning the minimum wage make $10 in one morning. To come to the United States means, for some Dominicans, that they can support their families better from hundreds of miles away than by working alongside them in the Dominican Republic. For those who bring their entire families to this country, the extra money might mean better lifestyles for the families.

In addition, the United States, even in the worst inner-city neighborhoods, can promise free education for children and decent homes with electricity and running water. While the weather may not be as pleasant year-round as it is in Santo Domingo—and the

Dominicans on a food line in May 1984, after riots closed down the city's food stores

Dominican Republic does have its share of dangerous hurricanes—New York City, the destination of most Dominican emigrants, has some of the best resources and social services in the world. For example, a child can go from grade school through college at the city's numerous affordable open-enrollment schools.

Aside from the obvious advantages of being able to afford the basic necessities in the United States, there are other inducements to emigrating to this country. Dominicans see American life as luxurious. They meet American tourists who are vacationing in the Dominican Republic and who seem to have money to burn. They

pick up satellite signals of American television shows and see that
Americans live with every modern convenience. And they hear
from relatives who have already ventured to the United States
about the money to be made and the indulgences to be found in
this country.

Chain Migration

Sometimes Dominicans immigrate to the United States as families, but more often they come as individuals. When one member of
a family starts the process of immigration alone, expecting to be
joined later by other relatives, he or she begins a chain migration.

One of the biggest reasons Dominicans come to the United
States is because they already know someone who is here.
Permanent residents of the United States can sponsor their immediate family members when those members apply for legal entry. A
woman can send for her husband or children—even her parents.
Then, perhaps, once her husband has become a permanent resident, he can send for his siblings. For each immigrant who comes
here, there is an estimated average of 80 immigrants who can follow him or her, through family sponsorships.

Most Dominican Americans live in just a few cities around the
United States, in neighborhoods with other Dominicans. Not only
are there family members to greet the Dominican once he arrives in
this country, but there is a whole Dominican society ready to welcome the new immigrant and ease him into life as an American.
When so many Dominicans have already ventured to a new home, it
may not be so frightening for the next traveler to risk the move to a

Three young
Dominican-
American boys
enjoy a bag of
cotton candy, a
true American
treat.

foreign country. Once they are here, however, many Dominicans discover that the United States is not as foreign as they thought.

American Invasion

Many aspects of American culture have already "invaded" the Dominican Republic, only serving to make life in the United States more attractive. Dominicans admire and copy American fashions, music, dances, language, consumption patterns, technology, sports, and architecture. The American political and economic systems are often cited by the ruling elite as models for a successful system. Dominican universities have been modeled on American schools. Even feminism and new roles for women are creeping into what was once a very traditional and conservative society.

One uniquely American activity has become so ingrained in Dominican culture that Dominicans can almost claim more participants per capita than Americans. When the United States sent the Marines to invade the Dominican Republic in 1916, the Marines took along more than just ammunition. They introduced the game of baseball. That game has since worked its way into the Dominicans' lifestyle and has become an integral part of their daily lives.

When a male child is born in the Dominican Republic, a father will celebrate the boy's birth by placing a baseball glove in his crib. Every day, after the men leave their work in the sugar mills and factories, they gather on baseball fields looking for pick-up games. Children often miss school to play the game. They make gloves out of milk cartons, balls from sewed-up socks, and bats from guava-tree limbs. The sport is so important that the Dominican Republic has its own baseball league, sponsored by the sugar industry, with games scheduled in the off-season from sugar harvesting.

The interesting result of this Dominican obsession with baseball has been that major-league baseball in the United States is filled with players recruited from the Dominican playing fields. Many dreams have been fulfilled by high-paying contracts from major-league teams. The Dominican town of San Pedro de Marcoris is famous for having contributed more major-league players per capita than any other place at any time.

Dominicans were first recruited to play American ball when Cuba's teams left the Caribbean leagues in the 1960s, after Fidel Castro came into power. Whereas United States teams once looked to talented young Cubans to fill out their ball clubs, they now actively recruit dozens of Dominican players. In fact, no baseball team in the United States is without at least one Dominican player, and twenty major ball clubs run full-scale camps on the outskirts of Santo Domingo. Dominican players already working in the United States often go back to the Dominican Republic in the off-season to keep playing in the Dominican league. To not return and give one's compatriots a chance to see one play would be a major insult from a Dominican American ballplayer.

Dominican players, who are generally smaller than their American counterparts, are trained to be good with a glove and to be switch-hitters with a powerful line drive, because they are usually not strong enough to hit one over the fence. Many Dominican players are shortstops, called *mediocampistas* in the Dominican

Republic, simply because their smaller stature makes them better infielders.

Baseball has become the means of escape for a class of kids who are forced to leave school at an early age in order to work and help support their families. The quality of their education, which is compulsory only to the age of 14, has been very low, and their average family income is just over $1,200 a year. By working in the cane fields for a few years, they become strong. Because they play year-round, their game is always sharp. They work hard to make the big leagues, having heard of the success of some of their

Baseball is so popular among Dominican Americans that children are given gloves and bats at a young age.

continued on page 44

Elvis García
A Dream of Your Own

Elvis García is ten years old and lives in Queens, New York,
with four brothers and sisters.

My mom and dad met in this country, so I was born here. I am a completely American citizen. Can you believe they named me Elvis? Actually, I kind of like it. They thought it was the ultimate American name.

My dad relied on the old customs when I was born, though. He put a small baseball mitt and ball in my crib. This was to guarantee that I would be a baseball player. I think he had already figured out that my two brothers weren't going to be famous ball players. I was the last hope. I haven't told him yet that I don't want to be a ball player, either. He's going to be really sad, so I'm just going to wait. I like it a lot for fun, but that's it. In the Dominican Republic it is a really big deal, you know. Even more so than in this country, if you can believe it. I have a cousin, Manny, who plays pro baseball in California. He is kind of everybody's idol because he makes a lot of money, and we watch him on TV. People are really poor in the Dominican Republic, and lots of Dominican Americans are poor here, too. So baseball is the big dream.

My big dream is to design computer games. I am really good in math and stuff. I can already design programs on the computer at school. I got advanced placement. That's the first time that has happened to anybody in my family. I am proud and so is my mom, I think. My oldest sister, too. She says I am going to be one of those computer geniuses you read about. You never know.

I really like living in Queens. My dad works with my Uncle Julio running a cab company. It took them a long time to do this, but now they are on their own. My mom likes it here, too. She cried sometimes because she missed her home country. Last year Dad gave her a ticket to the Dominican Republic as a Christmas present. She went for a visit and saw her sister and mother. She liked her visit a lot, and doesn't miss her home as much now that she's been back. She says she was imagining things were a lot better than they were. I guess missing things makes your imagination work like that.

We live near other people from the Dominican Republic. I speak Spanish. I like knowing two languages. I think this will help me one day, too. On weekends we have clubs that get together and play baseball. It's fun because it's for adults and kids and there's music playing and the moms bring food. Not in the winter, of course, because it's really cold here then.

I guess I'm going to have to tell my dad about the baseball thing pretty soon. Maybe he won't be as sad as I think. He's a good guy, and I think he would want me to be happy. He always says each of us should have a dream, that's why we came here. You know, even though I have never been to my parents' country, I think there are more dreams here than there.

countrymen who have become famous playing *beisbol* in the United States. The signing bonus, often as little as $2,500 for an American contract, is still more than twice a year's salary in the Dominican Republic.

Destination: Puerto Rico

Just 80 miles east of the Dominican Republic lies another island filled with Spanish-speaking Caribbean natives who have also been profoundly affected by American culture. But unlike Dominicans, these islanders are United States citizens. They are Puerto Ricans, and as inhabitants of a Commonwealth of the United States, they have American passports and all the other rights of United States citizenship.

Puerto Rico's history is similar to the Dominican Republic's. Once a Spanish colony, its residents still speak Spanish as their native language. Puerto Rico became a territory of the United States during the Spanish-American War at the turn of the century, not long before American Marines invaded the Dominican Republic.

Dominicans choose to go to Puerto Rico for many reasons. Because their backgrounds are similar, Dominicans feel comfortable living among Puerto Ricans. They don't feel like aliens, hailing from another country and speaking a different language. Instead, they blend in with Puerto Rican culture, the way a Canadian could easily blend into mainland United States culture.

In addition, because Puerto Rico is part of the United States, it is used by Dominicans as a stepping stone to living in a mainland city such as New York or Miami. Many Dominicans travel to Puerto Rico illegally, without obtaining the proper tourist visa first. They sneak into the island country and then establish themselves with new Puerto Rican identities. From there, they can travel to the United States unhindered, because there is no customs check between Puerto Rico and the mainland. No passports or identification are required. So once in Puerto Rico, a Dominican can fly easily to New York without fear of being stopped by the Immigration and Naturalization Service (INS).

Of course, since the distance between the Dominican Republic and Puerto Rico is very short, the decision to travel there first is an obvious one. But the distance can be deceiving. For many Dominicans, the journey to Puerto Rico can be long, difficult, and even deadly.

= 3 =

What Is Their Journey Like?

The Dangerous Waters of the Mona Passage

When Dominicans decide to brave the trip to Puerto Rico, most don't just hop on a cruise liner and arrive in San Juan, the capital, hours later. They make the journey as illegal travelers—illegal in the manner in which they leave the Dominican Republic and illegal in the manner in which they get into Puerto Rico. Once they settle in Puerto Rico, they are known as undocumented immigrants because their immigration was executed without proper documentation from the United States government.

The first thing a Dominican trying to get to Puerto Rico does is to find a smuggler. Someone who has the means to obtain a boat and who perhaps bribes the proper officials arranges for the person along with many other Dominicans to meet late at night at a departure point. Most of the boats, called *yolas,* leave from the northeast coast of the Dominican Republic, where the fishing villages are fringed by wooded hillsides that offer perfect hiding places until the boat or boats are ready. Hundreds of Dominicans wait in makeshift houses until the signal is given to board the boats. They wade through leech-filled swamps to reach a *yola,* and

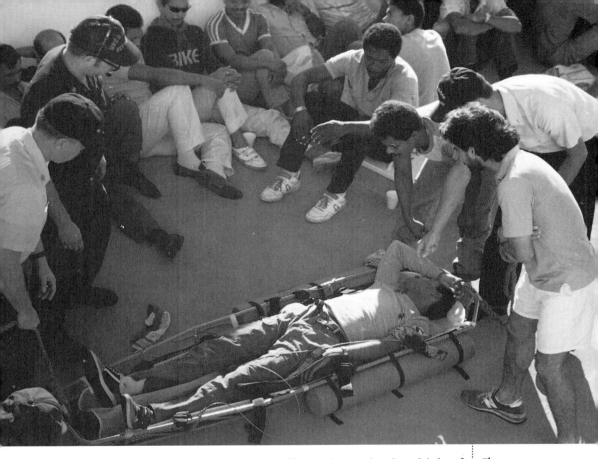

if they are lucky enough to board, set off in silence in the thick of the night. Those who are turned away are forced to find their way back alone and wait until the next opportunity to board a *yola,* perhaps days or weeks later.

For the services of a smuggler, Dominicans pay between $150 and $500, depending on how much work the smuggler will do for them. Higher prices are charged to those Dominicans who want passage from the shores of Puerto Rico overland to San Juan. The cheaper rates mean the immigrants will be left on the shores to fend for themselves. If an immigrant wishes to obtain passage all the way to New York City, complete with falsified papers, the

This man was picked up at sea by the U.S. Coast Guard from a yola and rushed to the hospital to be treated for severe stomach pains.

cost can be up to $10,000. For a Dominican, this can constitute the savings of a lifetime. Some Dominicans sell all their property, mortgage their homes, or borrow the money at 10 percent interest a month to buy the passage. Yet many never actually reach their destination the first time and are forced to scrounge for the money for a second, third, or fourth attempt at crossing the strait.

Most of the smugglers are part of organized crime rings in the Dominican Republic. The smugglers are called "consuls," a sarcastic reference to the American diplomats who are responsible for issuing legal immigration papers. The smugglers' assistants, who recruit the passengers, are known as *busons.* They receive about $50 for each emigrant they enlist.

Some of the supposed smugglers, however, are merely con artists who take the Dominicans' money and disappear. Sometimes the smugglers are even members of the Dominican military; they will take the money and then claim the seas are too rough for passage. Or they will sail around to the other side of the Dominican Republic and tell the passengers that it is Puerto Rico. The emigrants have no recourse in these cases, no one to whom they can complain to get their money back.

It is also not uncommon for the local officers of the Dominican navy to take up to a third of a consul's profits in exchange for turning their heads when the *yolas* leave the Dominican Republic. The government continually denies that the military is involved.

Dozens of Dominicans crowd onto the *yolas,* which are often just little wooden fishing boats equipped with small outboard motors—certainly not suitable craft for traveling across the Mona Passage. The boats are so crowded that the passengers take turns sitting during the 24-to-48-hour trip. The Mona Passage is where currents from the Atlantic Ocean and the Caribbean Sea collide, and it is best traversed in large, solid ships. On a good day, the swells on the water reach 5 feet. On a rough day, the waves are as high as 20 feet; and at all times, sharks patrol the waters in search of meals. The less-than-sturdy, overcrowded *yolas* are often no match for the turbulent strait.

Other emigrants take a less-traveled route, going to Puerto Rico via the French-Dutch island of St. Martin. Dominicans can travel there unchecked. From St. Martin, they can take a less dangerous and less congested water route to eastern Puerto Rico.

In December of 1988, one smuggler's boat was wrecked during the passage. The bodies of 14 of the passengers eventually washed up on the shores of Puerto Rico. The rest of the other dozens of passengers most likely were eaten by the sharks. In 1987, a similar shipwreck ended tragically just 20 miles off the coast of the Dominican Republic. As many as 150 Dominicans, mostly women, had boarded a 50-foot *yola.* Four miles out at sea, the boat's outboard motor exploded. Most of the passengers couldn't swim and drowned immediately. Others clung to empty gas containers, desperately swimming to reach shore. The rest drifted 16 more miles out to sea. When one survivor alerted the Dominican authorities, they refused to send a rescue helicopter. The man chartered a seaplane to locate survivors, but because the waters were too rough to land the plane, he could only watch in horror as the drifters were attacked by sharks. At least 70 people died that day.

Every day, Dominicans read about accidents like this, yet they are not deterred from undertaking the dangerous trip. Each one hopes that he or she will survive the passage. But the

continued on page 52

=≡ 49 ≡=

Agostín Trejo
Good Things Happen

Agostín Trejo is 26 years old. He works in a fish market in Providence, Rhode Island. (Partial translation of his narrative was provided by his fiancée, Carmela Barbuena.)

I have only been in this country for two years. I will try to speak English because I have been studying very hard, but Carmela will help me. She has already helped me much to adjust to this country. We are going to be married soon, but we have to figure out some immigration laws first. I am not legal. Carmela was born in this country, so she is a citizen. We think that will make it okay, but we are not sure. It is a hard situation to feel afraid for being somewhere.

It was difficult enough to come to this country; I lost my family in the attempt. We decided to leave for Puerto Rico together. We saved a long time to afford to pay the men who arrange boat transportation across the Mona Passage. It is about 80 miles across to Puerto Rico, but the ocean was rough and the boat too crowded. Something happened with the engine, and then we turned over. Sixty people started the journey, and twelve of us finished it. My mother, father, sister, and brother were not among the twelve. I cannot bear to think of what happened. The sharks came before another boat came by. It is only luck at all that I am here, if you can call losing your family luck. But enough of that. It is too much.

In Puerto Rico I was not myself. I am a good and decent person, but grief made me crazy. I didn't want to be on another island surrounded by ocean. I stole papers from someone in the airport and flew to New York. I was so afraid. I burned the papers as soon as I arrived here, afraid to even throw them away. I met a kind woman in New York at a restaurant. She told me her son had moved to Providence, Rhode Island. I liked the name. It sounded peaceful. So I moved.

It has been good for me here. I work for a Portuguese family in a fish market. The man says I do very good work, and he pays me well. This is not such a usual experience for Dominican Americans. The man's father came here from Portugal, so he understands how hard it is to succeed in a new land. And I met Carmela in the market! She came in one day shopping with her mother, and I knew immediately that she was the girl for me. I was very nice to her mother! Carmela came back the next day by herself, and we have been together ever since.

Carmela's family has taken me in like a son. This has lessened some of the pain I feel at my own loss. Her parents came here in 1968. They understand hardship and trying to make a better life. They didn't judge me for being illegal even though they themselves are now citizens.

It is funny how good things happen so soon after terrible things sometimes. We are going to have quite a wedding. The man I work for will make all the fish stew we can eat for his wedding gift. Carmela's family knows most of the Dominican community here, so it will be a big party. Carmela and I will dance all night. We will toast to a happy future in America. I know this would make my family proud.

Dominican Civil Defense estimates that in the 1980s, 40,000 to 50,000 Dominicans emigrated in *yolas* and at least 6,500 died trying. That makes the chances about one in seven that a *yola* passenger will not survive the trip, and this estimate has been cited by some as conservative. Many Dominicans who die in this way are never found. They leave their families, are never heard from again, and the families have no choice but to assume they are dead.

Upon Reaching Puerto Rico

The Dominican authorities, short of funds for patrolling for outbound boats, direct most of their resources toward trying to keep out Haitians, who are fleeing an even worse political and economic situation. It is usually the United States Border Patrol that catches the undocumented immigrants when they reach Puerto Rico, but even the Border Patrol's resources are limited to small boats and a rented plane. Undocumented immigrants caught arriving in Puerto Rico are usually just sent back to the Dominican Republic and kept in jail until they can pay a small fine for leaving the country illegally (about $70, just a fraction of the smugglers' fees). In 1990 alone, the Border Patrol deported almost 15,000 Dominicans from Puerto Rico.

Most new Dominican immigrants head for San Juan, the capital of Puerto Rico, which has a large Dominican population and offers more chances to find work. The resident Dominicans live in the working-class section of the San Juan metropolitan area known as Barrio Obrero, where they often own the area's small stores and restaurants, or in Santurce and Río Piedras. These two areas have been rebuilt by the large Dominican population. In San Juan and other cities, Dominicans find jobs as construction workers, domestic servants, waiters, mechanics, and other unskilled and semiskilled laborers. In the rural areas of Puerto Rico, Dominicans may take jobs harvesting beans on coffee plantations, a job native Puerto Ricans refuse to do.

Dominicans in Puerto Rico try to pass as native Puerto Ricans, often acquiring fake birth certificates to prove they were born there. With the false documents, they can easily disguise themselves as Puerto Ricans, who are United States citizens. But even without a birth certificate, a Dominican can easily travel to the United States mainland because travel from Puerto Rico to the U.S. is considered domestic and therefore not subject to a customs check.

Though many Dominicans make Puerto Rico their final desti-

These three Dominican cousins live near each other in New York City and enjoy an American lifestyle.

nation, still more work for years to save the money to go to the mainland, particularly to New York City. The airfare can cost several hundred dollars, so it often takes months or years to get together enough money to make the move. But for many, the chance to get to New York is worth the wait.

Waiting for a Visa

Of course, not every Dominican immigrant travels to the United States illegally. Thousands arrive each year with the proper documents issued by the INS. But the wait for these papers is often so long that many Dominicans will try to skip the process altogether.

The first document a potential immigrant needs is a visa. A visa tells the authorities in a country that a person has been approved to enter that country. In the United States, there are two main types of visas—immigrant and nonimmigrant. Dominicans immigrating here need the former, but they often use the latter improperly to get into the country.

A nonimmigrant visa is given to a tourist or to a temporary visitor traveling here to do business or go to school. This visa is always for a limited period of time, and if the visa expires, its owner must renew it or leave the country. Otherwise, the owner can be arrested and deported. In order to get a temporary visa, the person applying has to show that he or she is not a risk for overstaying the time limit. An applicant usually does that, in the case of a tourist visa, by showing a bank account with a substantial amount of money or the ownership of a house in the person's native country. This shows the American officials that the applicant has a reason to return to his or her home.

An immigrant visa is issued to a person who intends to live permanently in the United States. But in order for any immigrant to get permission to come here, the person has to be sponsored by someone already here, whether it be a potential employer or a relative. Until 1990, immigrants without sponsors could apply for immigrant visas, but a change in the law that year eliminated the provision for such applications. Now, applicants have to be categorized by their reasons for coming here, and then they are counted according to quotas for those categories. Quotas are limits that are established by the government as to how many people can come from each country and in each category.

The current quota rules were established in 1965 by the Immigration and Nationality Act. That act gave each country a quota of 20,000 people who could immigrate each year and set no quota for immigrants sponsored by immediate relatives in the United States. In 1990, the United States government adjusted the quotas, expanding them to over 25,000 but now including immediate relatives in the limits. The yearly quotas are divided into categories for relatives of permanent residents, workers and artists with "exceptional" or "extraordinary" ability, skilled workers, and other classifications by ability.

Most Dominicans are sponsored by relatives and obtain "family preference visas." Someone with a relative in the United States has a good chance of obtaining a visa because immigration laws since 1965 have favored the reunification of families. The rules for allowing people into the United States on their abilities are very strict, and only the wealthiest Dominicans have the education or

A street in the Washington Heights section of New York City, where the Dominican American population is greatest in the United States.

job training to qualify for visas in this manner. Middle-class Dominicans sometimes obtain these visas, but usually by taking a domestic-service job for which they are overqualified.

For a Dominican, the wait for a visa starts at the American consulate in Santo Domingo. Every morning, before dawn, applicants begin lining up outside the walls of the consulate. The line gets very long very quickly and, within a few hours, officials stop new applicants from joining the line. Some Dominicans never even get inside the compound walls before they are turned away. The words to a popular Dominican song, called "Seeking a Visa for My Dream," reflect the universal frustration with the long wait for a visa: "It's five in the morning . . . with one thousand papers to prove my solvency, it's hard to be sincere. . . . It's nine in the morning, my patience is wearing thin. Already today's quota for visas to make a dream come true is filled."

The consulate in Santo Domingo is the second busiest American consulate in the world, yet the population of the Dominican Republic is less than that of New York City. Every day, consulate officials interview between 300 and 350 visa applicants. Seventy percent of them are rejected. Many of them return to apply again, often several times. But the ones who are accepted can then take the 50-minute flight that American Airlines runs between Santo Domingo and San Juan. The flight is so well-known, in fact, that smugglers of undocumented immigrants jokingly call their *yolas* "double A's" after the airline.

Some Dominicans arrive with documents that indicate different lives than those they have actually lived. They may pose as students or invent wealthy relatives in the United States and so are granted visas that they would otherwise not qualify for under

continued on page 61

57

Rosa Bachleda
Not Just Black and White

Rosa Bachleda is 38 years old and lives in Chicago, Illinois.
She is married to an American.

I had no plans to come to America. It sometimes seems that everyone in this country assumes you are waiting anxiously in the Dominican Republic for just one thing—emigration to America. Now, it's true that I was waiting to leave. When I was 20 I left for school in Guadalajara, Mexico. I couldn't wait to leave the island for a real future.

I was studying architecture but soon discovered that it was too limiting. I gradually moved to psychology and art. Even though I don't have a degree in Art Therapy, I think of myself as leaning that way. I lived rather communally in Mexico with a group of artists, political activists, therapists, and all sorts of people from a very international community. My first boyfriend there was from Italy, my second from Spain. I hope I am not breaking too many preconceived ideas for you about Dominicans and, well, Mexico, for that matter!

Mexico was a good place for me to be. I eventually moved to a lake town north of Guadalajara, where my friends and I joined together in an environmental movement to save the lake from pollution. It was incredible. We gave theater productions, had art shows, put out newsletters. It worked! But enough of Mexico—you want to know about America and me.

Well, I met my husband, Loren Bachleda, about the time of the environmental work. He was a visiting art professor from the Chicago Art Institute. We fell in love, and the next thing you know I'm married and living in Chicago. It's funny. My move to Mexico was so easy because of the language. My move to the United States was very difficult. Not just the language, either. Thank God for my husband.

The first thing I discovered here was that I was not black or white. This is something I had given very little thought to at home or in Mexico. But in Chicago, I was black to white America; I was some strange Spanish-speaking person to black America. I am not saying I was ill-treated. My husband's group of friends welcomed me warmly. But I felt very out of place—homeless, really. It is better now, but I have been here six years.

I met many artists through Loren. I was looking to find a place in this community and feeling a strange racial displacement. This is when I decided to try to bring together black and white women artists to discuss racial divisions and create art work about this topic. Oh, it sounds pretty easy, but it has been five years of work. There was not too much trust among the women at first, but eventually we were all able to talk and argue and accuse and become friends and make art. The name of our group is Not Just Black and White. We have had two shows and recently published a book of our art works and writings. I am very gratified by our success. I am even more gratified by our personal growth.

This work has made being in Chicago very worthwhile to me. I feel that I have learned about myself as a biracial woman and have contributed to the healing of this country that I have adopted somewhat uneasily.

Of course I miss my family, but Loren and I are a family now. We are connected to our community of friends here in Chicago much as I was to my community in Mexico. We don't have children, but finally we think we might be ready. I guess I trust being here and the future of this society enough to welcome a child.

Loren enjoys our trips to the Dominican Republic, and since he speaks Spanish, my parents enjoy him. It is always good to be back on the farm and to relax with an easier way of life. Yet, I have no illusions about returning one day. My life is here. So be it.

stringent American laws. However, the majority wait patiently until they qualify for the proper documents needed to go to their destination in the United States. Usually, that destination is New York City.

Destinations on the Mainland

Dominican Americans who don't settle in Puerto Rico have a whole country of destinations to choose from, but most of them go to the same small neighborhood in New York City. In northern Manhattan, centered around the main thoroughfare of West 162nd Street, is the area known as Washington Heights. It runs right up against the George Washington Bridge, above Harlem. Once inhabited by Irish, Jewish, and German immigrants, it is now populated largely by Dominican Americans. In fact, more immigrants come to New York from the Dominican Republic than from any other country, and New York has the highest concentration of Dominicans outside of the Dominican Republic.

In the late 1980s and early 1990s, Dominican Americans began settling more in other American cities. Drawn by an enormous Latino population, Dominicans have been establishing major enclaves in Miami. Dominicans can also be found living in Chicago; Boston, and other Massachusetts cities; Providence, Rhode Island; and New Jersey. But New York is still the primary destination of Dominicans moving to the mainland United States.

Aside from Washington Heights, Dominicans can be found in smaller numbers in other neighborhoods around New York City. In Manhattan, they can be found in Spanish Harlem, longtime home to New York's Hispanic population, and the Lower East Side. In the outer boroughs, Dominicans live in the South Bronx, the Greenpoint section of Brooklyn, and the Jackson Heights section of Queens.

Becoming a Citizen

For many immigrants to the United States, the greatest moment of their lives is when they are sworn in as American citizens. But the road to citizenship is long, and many Dominican Americans choose never to follow it.

In order to become a naturalized United States citizen, an immigrant must first become a permanent resident. When a foreigner is granted an immigrant visa, he or she automatically qualifies for a permanent resident card, or "green card," which is received within a few months of arrival in the United States. The green card entitles the immigrant to legally work and live in this country but not to vote or hold an American passport. The holder must report to the INS once a year, providing a current address each time.

After five years of living permanently in the United States (or three years if the immigrant is married to an American citizen), a green card holder can apply for citizenship. Application for citizenship involves many long and confusing forms that can be difficult for someone who is not familiar with the system. After applying, the immigrant is contacted by the INS to take a citizenship test. The exam tests knowledge of United States history and government, and proficiency in reading and writing English.

If the immigrant passes the exam, he or she is sworn in as a citizen of the United States. The oath includes a promise to uphold the Constitution, much like the oath the President takes to hold office. Once an immigrant becomes a citizen, he or she can then throw away the green card, vote, hold certain government jobs, and carry an American passport.

The Grace of Amnesty

In 1986, Congress passed a law that made a special exception for certain undocumented immigrants who wanted to become permanent residents of the United States. The immigrants were granted amnesty for having broken the law when coming into this country illegally. *Amnesty* means "a pardon for an offense against a government." In this case, the government was willing to overlook the illegal entry and give the immigrants a fresh start.

Anyone who could prove that he or she had been living in the country without interruption for at least five years was automatically given a green card. The United States government was trying to solve the problem of undocumented immigration by starting again from scratch. But government officials weren't prepared for the hordes of people who actually qualified for permanent residency under the new law. Hundreds of thousands flocked to INS processing centers to file their applications.

Many of the applicants were Dominicans. For the undocumented immigrants, this new status meant no more fake names and social security numbers, no fear of deportation. Instead, they were now legal immigrants, and could work without dreading an employer who would turn them in to immigration officials.

However, not all undocumented immigrants in the United States had been living here long enough to meet the requirements for amnesty. Others could not prove that they did qualify, though they had lived here for more than five years. Undocumented immigrants are very careful not to give themselves away, so they mask their existence and hesitate to keep any revealing documents. Consequently, the ever-resourceful smugglers began manufacturing the appropriate documents to sell to potential immigrants who wanted a quick way to get a green card. They produced fraudulent receipts, checks, letters—anything that could show continuous residency for five years leading up to the law. Of course, the price for these fake documents ranged into the thousands of dollars.

As permanent residents, these newly legalized immigrants could legally send for their families through family-preference visas. The rush to bring in relatives was so great, in fact, that by 1990 the United States government had created a separate quota category just for the relatives of amnesty recipients. Realizing that the first amnesty law could not possibly have solved the entire undocumented problem since it ignored the families of the immigrants already living here, officials created the quota to (it was hoped) wipe the slate clean once and for all.

Those who applied for a visa under the separate category were not subject to the long waiting lists for a normal family-preference visa or an immigrant visa based on work status. But each year the quota for relatives of amnesty recipients soon reached its limit, and even many people applying under those provisions were forced to wait until they could be part of the next year's quota.

Part II

In the United States

Prejudices and Opportunities

Stereotypes in a New York Neighborhood

When Dominican Americans choose to live grouped together in one area of a city, as they do in Washington Heights or Spanish Harlem, they gain the benefits of being surrounded by familiar sounds, smells, and culture. Then, as a coherent ethnic group, Dominican Americans help new Dominican immigrants become adjusted to unfamiliar surroundings and work together to build power against other interest groups in the community. One disadvantage of living in tightknit groups is that non-Dominicans tend to stereotype Dominicans based on a few short encounters with some.

The stereotype that Dominican Americans have the hardest time shaking is the one that depicts all Dominicans in Washington Heights as drug dealers. Washington Heights was once a run-down neighborhood complete with abandoned buildings and garbage strewn about the sidewalks. The influx of the Dominican American population since the 1960s revived the area after earlier residents began moving out to the suburbs. But Washington Heights still has a very high crime rate and the heaviest drug traffic in New York City, and some of the dealers are Dominican Americans.

Drug customers from suburban areas cross the nearby George Washington Bridge to purchase crack, cocaine, and heroin. Some Dominican Americans who admit to having sold drugs say that pressures from their families back in the Dominican Republic to succeed in the United States led them to begin selling drugs. It was the only job they could get that would pay them enough money to send some home and still be able to survive New York's skyrocketing cost of living. One Dominican explained to a *New York Times* reporter that he had been unemployed and actively looking for work for months when he began dealing in order to avoid being evicted from his apartment.

Dominican Americans claim that New Yorkers, particularly

A Hispanic police officer patrols in New York City.

the police, have come to assume that all Dominican Americans they encounter are pushers. They say that they are scorned by non-Dominicans or mistreated by the police, who often don't look past the ethnic background. Dominicans contend that the police often detain them randomly and show a general lack of sensitivity toward Dominican American culture and attitudes.

Currently New York's police force is only 13 percent Hispanic, far below the proportion of Latinos in the New York population. The city government is trying to remedy the situation by revising the height and weight for police officers. One major reason there are so few Hispanics on the force is because many of them are just too small to meet the size specifications set by the department. Lowering the height and weight levels set by the department might make more Hispanics eligible to become New York City police officers.

Anger and Unrest

In 1992, the Dominican Americans' anger over mistreatment by police came to a head during the confusion that followed a Washington Heights shooting. On July 3rd of that year, a plain-clothes police officer named Michael O'Keefe shot José Garcia, a Dominican immigrant, in the stomach and back during an arrest. Garcia died from his wounds. Immediately, questions arose as to the circumstances surrounding the shooting.

Witnesses said that O'Keefe, without being provoked, beat Garcia with a police radio and then shot the unarmed man. The police, however, contested that Garcia had attacked O'Keefe and then pulled out a .38 caliber pistol. The police then said that the known drug offender had tried to flee from them. The gun was later recovered.

The incident was followed by six days of disturbances in Washington Heights. Dominican American demonstrators who were angry over the shooting threw trash cans, bottles, and rocks; they broke windows, looted stores, and destroyed police cars. Encompassing 60 square blocks of northern Manhattan, the riots led to 139 arrests, 90 injuries (including 74 injuries to police officers), and one death. Fourteen buildings caught fire and 121 vehicles were damaged. Mayor David N. Dinkins visited several times with the Garcia family and with neighborhood residents to try to bring some peace to the situation, and Cardinal John O'Connor pleaded with the mostly Roman Catholic neighborhood to maintain calm.

In the months that followed the rioting, city officials tried to prepare Dominican Americans for any decision that might come from the grand jury on whether or not to charge O'Keefe. They held special workshops to explain the grand jury system, which only decides if there is enough evidence to charge someone with a crime, not the actual guilt or innocence of the person. There are no grand juries in the Dominican Republic, so the meetings were meant to introduce the mostly immigrant population to the differences in the two countries' systems. They also explained the difficulty in getting an indictment against a police officer.

During the grand jury hearings, O'Keefe testified that Garcia was located outside a building that was known to police as a drug location. He noted that Garcia had a bulge in his waistband that suggested he was carrying a gun. Garcia tried to flee, then turned

continued on page 75

Rafael Guarnizo
Straight Talk

Rafael Guarnizo is 40 years old and lives in Manhattan. He is a self-employed accountant.

Listen, I'm going to be honest about everything. Even about how angry I am at this country. Even about some of the illegal things my family have done. I no longer see the point of talking if you are not going to be truthful. There are too many problems in the world today to hide behind being nice. Okay?

Let's start with my brother. My brother helped to raise me, to feed my family, to put me through college. Things were very hard for my family when we moved here. My brother was already a young man when we moved here, but he had no schooling. He saw to it that I went to school. He couldn't find work. He honestly tried, that much I remember. He became a drug dealer. He made a lot of money. He made it possible for me to have the life I have now. I can say this openly because he moved back to the Dominican Republic several years ago with a lot of money and now has a quiet, nice life.

This is difficult because it fits right into all the stereotypes that people have about Dominican Americans and drugs, especially in Washington Heights. I am not saying he was right to do what he did; I am just saying he did what he thought was right. People get so angry at our community because of the drugs, but who do they think is buying? Take a look at the situation. It is all those young people with a little money in the suburbs who come here to buy. So why is it just our fault?

Another thing: Americans get upset because we come here in the first place. Do they not realize the economic and political disaster that the Dominican Republic is in? Would they not do the same? Do they not see the part the United States played in our political mess with interventions and support of dictators? It is too complicated to explain in a short time, but I'm just saying, take a good look before you make judgments.

Plus, people act as if we are coming to this paradise and ruining it. Please. Look at New York City. Do you think we created all the urban problems people are facing? Do you think we created racism? I think the racial tensions in this country are far worse than in mine. I didn't even know I was considered black until I came to the United States.

Okay. I just needed to say that. On the other hand, I have my own accounting firm in this country, and that would never have happened in the Dominican Republic. No way. I try to give back some of what I have learned, some of my prosperity, by working closely with the Dominican community here, providing accounting services to new businesses. I have strong ties to the community. I read the local cultural magazines (like *Aha!*), patronize the local restaurants and stores, and am currently active in a political organization to help make the needs of the community known to the city. This is, I suppose, the American way—to try to give back what you have received.

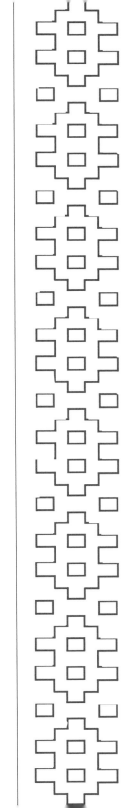

For all my frustration with being a black American, a Dominican American, I am still glad to be raising my children in New York, where so much is available to them. My wife runs one of the day care centers for Alianza Dominicana. She sees every day the young children and how their lives have been made better by their parents' courage in coming here. So you see, it is not all anger on my part, although the anger is put to good use, I think.

In the end, although my brother is the one person my family is most ashamed to recognize, he is the one person to whom I am most grateful. It's a strange world, isn't it?

＊　＊　＊

to attack O'Keefe, pulling the pistol from his waistband. O'Keefe fired twice. The grand jury ruled the death a justifiable homicide and declined to charge O'Keefe. Following the decision, police beefed up their presence in Washington Heights, but little unrest occurred.

The Political Solutions

Dominican Americans in New York have begun to act through means other than violent demonstrations against what they feel is unjust treatment. They have organized community service groups and have tried to elect city officials who are sympathetic to their needs and complaints. Politically, they must compete for important government seats against other well established interest groups, but Dominican Americans' power is slowly growing within city government.

In 1991, changes to the district divisions for Manhattan created city government districts that are dominated by minority voters. One such area is primarily filled with Dominican Americans and now provides the Dominicans with a way to put a voice in city government. But Dominicans have traditionally had trouble getting that voice.

Hispanics make up one fourth of New York's population and more than 77 percent of the Washington Heights population. Yet less than half of the Latinos in New York are registered to vote. Among Dominican Americans, the percentage of registered voters is dramatically lower. The majority of Dominican Americans are not yet United States citizens and are therefore not eligible to

On July 7, 1992,
Police officers
were called in to
quell disturbances
in Washington
Heights after an
officer shot and
killed a Domini-
can American.

vote; many are undocumented immigrants who cannot legally become citizens.

On the other hand, Puerto Ricans are American citizens by birth and can register to vote in New York. In addition, for decades they have been (and continue to be) the largest Hispanic group in that city. As a result, Puerto Ricans have dominated Hispanic politics in New York. In Washington Heights and Spanish Harlem, Dominican Americans are often represented by Puerto Rican elected officials.

This union has upset some Dominican Americans. They feel that the Puerto Ricans have their own agenda and do not adequately represent the Dominicans and their interests. Tensions between the two ethnic groups have surfaced.

The tension begins in Puerto Rico, where native Puerto Ricans resent Dominican immigrants. The Puerto Ricans accuse

the Dominicans of contributing to population growth, wage reduc-
tions, and abuse of public services. They say the Dominicans take
jobs away from Puerto Ricans. But studies have shown that the
Dominicans don't compete with the natives for the well-paying
jobs. The positions they usually take are those that the Puerto
Ricans refuse to do. In addition, the majority of undocumented
Dominicans in Puerto Rico do not receive government services.

The tensions between the two ethnic groups in New York
date back to the days when Dominicans first immigrated to the
United States. At the time Dominicans began arriving, Puerto
Ricans had been living in New York for a generation and consti-
tuted one of the largest Hispanic groups in the city. But as
Dominicans moved in, Puerto Ricans moved on. The children of
the Puerto Ricans who had owned most of the Hispanic businesses in the city had gone on to become doctors and lawyers and
other professionals. Some had moved out to the suburbs. Most of
the Puerto Ricans in New York were second- or third-generation
New Yorkers who had no interest in taking over the family businesses. So the immigrant Dominicans started buying into those
businesses.

Some of those businesses have been brought back from
near collapse. Dominicans say that the Puerto Ricans never
realized their full potential and that the Dominicans will be
more successful in New York. The Puerto Ricans, on the other
hand, accuse Dominicans of coming to the United States solely
to collect welfare.

Of course, both of these images are inaccurate, but they
reflect the kinds of prejudices that have arisen between the two
groups because they are forced to vie for power under the one eth-

A bodega in New York City owned by a Dominican American. Many Dominicans save establishments from collapse when the children of Puerto Rican entrepreneurs refuse to work the family businesses.

nic heading of "Hispanic." Dominican Americans have accused some Puerto Rican politicians and community leaders of failing to reach out to the Dominican American population. Many of the Hispanic community groups were started by Puerto Ricans but now help Dominicans, yet others will serve the Dominican American community but won't appoint Dominicans to the leadership posts. So Dominican Americans now have their own community organization.

Alianza Dominicana has been a prominent force in the Dominican community since 1982. The Alianza was formed specifically to help the growing population of Dominican immigrants in Washington Heights. Aimed primarily at children and families,

Alianza Dominicana works to provide alternatives and solutions to the violence and poverty that plague the area's residents. The organization runs a community center, a family counseling program to prevent and end family violence and abuse, a citizenship assistance program to help with the complicated INS process, an immunization and health program, a school dropout prevention project, an employment and training center, a drug-treatment program, and day-care services. The Alianza also sponsors regular cultural events. All these and other services are available through several locations to the estimated 150,000 Dominicans living in northern Manhattan.

A Different Take on Things

One of the reasons Dominican Americans are not as involved in politics as Puerto Ricans is their general mistrust of the political system. Politics is just one of the things that is perceived differently in the Dominican Republic than it is in the United States, and the differences in perception are not always easily changed.

In the Dominican Republic, politics and politicians are perceived to be corrupt, as are the police, the military, and the court system. So it is not hard to understand why Dominican Americans mistrust the motives of the police and the government. Officials in the Dominican Republic are allegedly easily bribed or manipulated.

But most problems for Dominican Americans stem from racial differences. The people of the Dominican Republic are generally of mixed races. Descendants of European (Spanish) Caucasians intermarried with descendants of black slaves and migrants from Haiti. Dominicans have a distinctive black or mulatto Hispanic physical appearance, but their skin color can range from olive to very dark.

In the Dominican Republic, there is a strong prejudice against dark-skinned blacks. In fact, the word *black* is reserved for describing Haitians and is separate in meaning from *Dominican*. The words *Haitian* and *black* are used with contempt by many Dominicans. Politicians openly voice racial slurs, though many of them take pains to mask their own dark skin. (Trujillo went so far as to wear makeup to lighten his appearance while publicly warning of the "corrupting influence" of interracial marriages.) Mixed-blood Dominicans must even have their passports stamped *Indian*. But few Dominicans themselves would receive mistreatment for their darker skin. They feel they are not black, since they are still not as dark as Haitians.

In the United States, there are no subtleties of race divisions. One is either black or white, and a Hispanic can be either. Many darker-skinned Dominican Americans face racial prejudice for the first time in the United States. And many native-born Americans don't know what to make of this odd type of black person who speaks Spanish. The transition from being a member of a dominant racial group to being categorized not only as a minority but as a racial minority that includes people with whom Dominicans would not want to be categorized makes adjusting to life in the United States even more difficult for Dominican immigrants. Some respond with defensiveness; others return to the Dominican Republic with a new perception of "black is beautiful."

Finding a Job

For Dominican Americans, especially undocumented immigrants, finding a job that compares in status to the one they held in the Dominican Republic can be very difficult. Though one would think that it is the undocumented immigrants who have less skills and education, they are usually the ones who must take the greatest reduction in rank from the jobs for which they are qualified. That is because in the United States mainland, undocumented Dominican immigrants are usually visa abusers. They have overstayed a tourist visa, which they could only obtain by proving they had a good job and middle-class economic status in the Dominican Republic. Up to one

A group of Dominican men in which many races are represented.

third of the 30,000 tourist visas issued each year for Dominicans are abused. Or the Dominicans have falsified papers, which cost them a lot of money—money only available to those Dominicans who held somewhat decent jobs in the Dominican Republic. These immigrants were usually white-collar workers in their native country.

The legal immigrants are usually those who obtained immigrant visas through family sponsorship and did not have to provide any financial statements to the immigration officials. They are more likely to have held low-paying jobs or to have been unemployed in the Dominican Republic.

The average Dominican American has only about nine years of education. Of course, those who were professionals and white-collar workers in the Dominican Republic have many more years of education to their credit. Yet Dominican Americans work almost exclusively in blue-collar jobs in the United States. A mere 13 percent of the men and less than 3 percent of the women are professionals. Only a handful more are managers or clerks. The majority of Dominican Americans—80 percent overall—work in factories or in the service industry (in hotels, restaurants, and private homes).

For the undocumented immigrants, there is no choice but to take the lower-status jobs. Since 1986, it has been illegal in the United States to hire anyone who is not a United States citizen or who does not have a green card or a work visa. Many employers fear being prosecuted for breaking the law and refuse to hire undocumented workers into higher profile positions. Undocumented workers are only offered blue-collar jobs, especially those jobs for which the employer can take advantage of the immigrant's fear of being deported. The firms for which the immigrants work are more often small Dominican-owned companies in which the sense of community protects the undocumented workers' status but in which the companies remain competitive by denying their workers certain basic benefits. At such companies the workers are least likely to learn of their rights according to United States laws.

For the documented immigrants, who often has minimal education, the service and manufacturing jobs are the only ones for which they are qualified. Their lack of job skills and little knowledge of English severely limit their ability to obtain any clerical or managerial positions.

Women's Changing Roles

It is not just racial attitudes and job status that must change when a Dominican moves to the United States. Gender attitudes are different, too, as Dominican American women find themselves taking on new roles in both the family and the community.

In the Dominican Republic, married women traditionally do not work outside the home. They spend their days working as wives and mothers and are supported by means of their husbands' salaries, though some women have been forced by economic circumstances to go to work in low-skilled factory jobs. And when a Dominican woman doesn't work, she usually submits to her husband's decisions about the family and the family finances. Single women do work—as nurses, teachers, secretaries, or in other traditionally feminine occupations. Most Dominican women, however, do not usually attend college.

Dominican women who emigrate to Puerto Rico go there to elevate their social position. They do this by making more money. But the irony is that in order for Dominican women to make money in Puerto Rico, they usually have to take jobs that are beneath their qualifications. They work as domestic servants or waitresses, even though they are trained to work in hospitals, schools, or offices. The jobs for which the women are qualified are not available to them in Puerto Rico as undocumented immigrants, though Dominican men can more often take on better skilled, higher paying positions as mechanics, carpenters, or tailors. In addition, as Dominican women in Puerto Rico, they tend to suffer sexual, racial, and class discrimination from native Puerto Ricans.

Additionally, precisely because they have taken the initiative to migrate to Puerto Rico, these Dominican women tend to be less passive and dependent. By making the move to a new country,

A Dominican American teenager works in a minimum wage job to help support her family.

they automatically begin to dispel cultural standards which place
them in positions inferior to men.

On the United States mainland, this movement toward
equality is even more evident. American feminism makes its way
into Dominican American life when Dominican women choose to
work. They make this choice partly out of necessity because
more and more American families need two incomes to survive,
but also because they want to make a better life for their children. They want their children, both girls and boys, to eventually
go to college and become members of the middle class. They contribute to the finances of the family and therefore to some of the
major decisions.

As a result, Dominican American husbands are much more
likely than their counterparts in the Dominican Republic to share
the responsibilities at home of cleaning the house and caring for
the children, to recognize the value of women, and to acknowledge their sacrifices. Yet the housework responsibilities are not
totally equal in a Dominican American home, because such an
arrangement is considered by both men and women to be lacking
in manliness.

The Women in Charge

Another changing aspect of Dominican American women's
lives is seen in the increasing number of women who are heads of
households. More and more Dominican women are raising entire
families on their own. In fact, more than 40 percent of Dominican
households in the United States are headed by women.

Sometimes this shift in responsibility is caused by a failed marriage, a phenomenon that increases for Dominicans when they move to the United States. Some experts have concluded that it is the changing roles of women which cause the marriage bonds to weaken, reasoning that as women become more independent, the need for family solidarity is lessened.

Unfortunately, Dominican American women who head households also have a high rate of public assistance. As many as one in four Dominican American households collects welfare or food stamps. This probably reflects the inability of Dominican American women to secure jobs in the United States that pay enough for them to support their families and to pay someone to look after their children while they are away. Though Dominican American women work, they appear not to be working in very high-paying jobs.

Dominican American women work predominantly in the garment industry. More than 40 percent of the Dominican women in New York work sewing in factories. And the conditions in these factories are notoriously poor. The women are paid by the piece, and quotas for completed work are kept high while piece wages are kept low. In fact, the average hourly wage for an employee in one of these factories actually *fell* between 1965 and 1980. Known as sweatshops, the factories employ many undocumented immigrants and exploit them by taking advantage of their fear of deportation. The employees are expected to work long hours and they are given only short breaks for lunch and dinner.

But the women who do take these jobs have little choice. They are usually lacking education, and because many of them

Over forty percent of Dominican American women are heads of households and raise entire families on their own.

have immigrated illegally, they are not allowed by law to work in the United States. Employers threaten to tell authorities about the undocumented immigrants if they do not comply with the conditions of employment. Few of these women belong to unions—first because they know little about the unions' existence, and second because they fear being discovered and deported—so they have no recourse against unfair employers.

The Limitations of Living in the United States

One of the reasons Dominican women work is to help their families save the money they need to return to the Dominican Republic. A majority of Dominican Americans express some desire to move back to their homeland when they have earned enough money to live comfortably there. But there are circumstances that end up limiting their ability to return.

First of all, life in the United States is expensive, especially in New York City. Though salaries are as much as 20 times more in New York than they are in Santo Domingo, expenses quickly eat up most of this extra income. One man's living costs in Washington Heights were categorized in *The New York Times* recently: Of the $1,000 or so the man makes each month cleaning offices, $212 pays his rent, $175 pays for meals, $300 goes into savings, and $300 goes to his wife and children in the Dominican Republic.

Basically, this man is paying to live two lives—one as a New Yorker and one as the father and husband in the Dominican

Republic. He never enjoys a night out or even a movie. Each year he budgets $500 for airfare home.

And he is one of the few who has a savings account. Most Dominican Americans cannot afford to stash anything away for the day they intend to return to their homes. They are too busy trying to earn enough to cover their bills and pay off the thousands of dollars they borrowed to pay smugglers to come here. If they don't pay the smugglers back in the Dominican Republic, they fear their families will be thrown out of their homes. Many who planned to be only temporary migrants to the United States soon discover that they have settled here for

An international phone center (for calling out of the country) in Washington Heights serves the many men and women who call their families still living in the Dominican Republic.

continued on page 93

Carmen Emilia Rodríguez
My Own Music

Carmen Emelia Rodríguez is 30 years old. She lives in Boston with her six-year-old daughter, her sister, and four-year-old nephew. She works as a hotel maid.

I have been in Boston five years. I moved here with my husband, Pedro. We separated a couple of years ago because I could not take the life of a musician anymore. We lived in New York City when we first came to this country. His brother was there, so we were able to come legally. That is rare these days. Most people I know are here illegally. It is hard either way.

Anyway, we moved to Boston so that my husband could be in a well-known merengue band. You know this music? It is very popular in Latino communities and sometimes outside of those, too. You maybe know *440*? That is that band with Juan Luis Guerra. He is really good. Anyway, we moved here and things went very well with this band called *Mona*—named after the Mona Passage between the Dominican Republic and Puerto Rico. It was too much. He was always gone and out late and there was alcohol and, well, I don't want to talk about all the women who hang around bands. Finally, enough was enough and I moved out. Back home, I think I would have just stayed with him forever because that is what women do. But here, I had a choice. I know lots of women who are alone with their children.

My sister, Yesenia, is one of them. Her situation was different. She was living in New York until last year. There was a lot of violence in that home, let me tell you. This is something our community does not like to talk about—men hitting women. But it happens. There is a group of Dominican women in Washington Heights in New York who run a center for women like this. They talk to people in the community and encourage women to get help. Yesenia did. Finally, when she could see it would not be better, she took her little boy and moved here with me. I am glad to have her. We help each other out a lot.

My Pedro was not like Yesenia's husband. We have our differences, but he still pays me money for our daughter every month and visits with her when he is in town. This makes life so much easier for us. Yesenia and I both work as maids at the same hotel in Boston. It's not so much money, but to tell you the truth, it is a pretty good job. I don't have so much education, and at least you are alone to clean without someone looking over you all the time. My best friend in New York works in a factory, and it is just about killing her.

My parents are still in the Dominican Republic. They finally moved out of Santo Domingo and into the country with my uncle, so their life is much better now. I try to save some little money every month to send to them. It is not much, but a little helps a lot back home.

Yesenia and I sometimes think to go back, but the fact is I think we have become too independent to return to the old ways. We can work here and get along fine, thank you. This is kind of a surprise. We like it. We think our children will have a better life in Boston than back home—or in New York, actually.

So for now it is just the two immigrant sisters in Boston making a new life. As I say to Pedro, I can make my own music now!

✳   ✳   ✳

good and that it is unlikely that they will ever return to the Dominican Republic.

For others, it is not necessarily the money that stops them from returning but the sense of permanence they have acquired in the United States. When entire families migrate and no one is left in the Dominican Republic, the desire to return home lessens. When children are born and raised in the United States, there is even more reason to stay. Most second-generation Dominican Americans do not have the sense of loyalty to the Dominican Republic that their parents have, and they feel little desire to abandon the place they have called home for their entire lives in order to live the dream their parents have arranged for them.

In addition, the education they have acquired here would qualify them for higher level jobs in the Dominican Republic. But the economy of that country could not support the return of so many educated workers. There are no jobs for them, so they would be returning to the life of destitution that their parents tried to escape.

Of course, not every Dominican American fails to realize the dream of returning wealthy and triumphant. Many Dominicans who have lived the majority of their lives in the United States do go back to their homeland when they retire. Taking substantial American pensions and Social Security payments, they build their dream houses and live off retirement incomes that, in the Dominican Republic, make them wealthy people.

═ **5** ═

Lifestyles

Working for a Living

T he typical Dominican American's day starts with the trip to work. In Washington Heights, that could mean a trip across the George Washington Bridge to New Jersey. There, Dominicans clean rooms in hotels or sew pants in factories or fix lights in office buildings. Most of the industries that employ Dominican Americans who work in blue-collar jobs are in northern or central New Jersey, just a stone's throw away from where they live in northern Manhattan.

The day is usually long, sometimes as much as fifteen hours, and the pay is minimal. The mean Dominican wage is only about three fifths of what the average New York city dweller makes. But on payday, most first-generation Dominican Americans can be found in one place—the *remesadoras*.

A *remesadora* is a money-transfer office from which Dominicans send part of their wages to their relatives in the Dominican Republic. These offices are responsible for the hundreds of millions of dollars sent from New York to Santo Domingo. And other *remesadoras* in Miami, Newark, Providence, and Boston have similar activity.

Many Americans assume that the undocumented immigrants come to this country to take advantage of government social ser-

vices. But in fact, among all undocumented Dominicans in the United States, more than 95 percent never receive welfare, unemployment benefits, or food stamps. The majority pay federal taxes and social security and regularly file their tax forms. They use a relative's social security number (which is only available to legal residents) or just make one up. Of course, with a fake number, they cannot receive a refund or collect social security when they get older. But many undocumented immigrants believe they will look better to officials in case they are caught if they show that they have followed the law.

One of the many Dominican American street peddlers in New York City who make a living selling food from a cart to passersby.

The Students

For younger Dominican Americans, a typical day means school. But in New York City, the enormous influx of Dominican children is putting a strain on the public school system. In just the first three years of the 1990s, 23,000 new Dominican students entered the New York City school system, more than twice as many as the next highest immigrant group. Many of the schools in the ethnic neighborhoods have become overcrowded. They are now filled to one and a half times what they were built to accommodate.

Some New Yorkers, however, see the new tide of immigrants as bringing life to a dying school system. In recent decades, many American families have moved out of the city to the suburbs in what has been called a middle-class exodus. The Dominicans and other immigrants who move in to replace the departing families refill the schools with new generations of eager young students who most likely will stay in the United States and become hard-working members of the community.

The New Hispanic Entrepreneurs

Though some Dominican Americans express a desire to return eventually to the Dominican Republic, the majority of Dominican Americans don't want to go back, particularly because their roots in the United States have become so strong. There is a large community of Dominican American business owners in New York who have established themselves as an important part of the

Dominican business owners operate all sorts of stores in cities around the country. This man owns and operates a flower shop in Manhattan.

New York Hispanic community. The Dominican Business Association estimates that Dominican Americans own about 9,000 small businesses in New York City alone.

One of the reasons some Dominican Americans find New York City so expensive is that they are saving their money to buy small businesses. Many of the traditionally Hispanic businesses in New York that were once owned by Puerto Ricans are now owned by Dominican Americans. Within a few years of their first arrival in large numbers in the 1960s and 1970s, Dominicans began buying most of the *bodegas* (small Hispanic grocery stores) and livery cab companies, as well as the restaurants that once had served Spanish Caribbean food from Cuba or Puerto Rico. They dominate these industries as the former owners retire without children who are interested in running the family businesses. Dominican immigrants now own 70 percent of all the *bodegas* and 90 percent of the gypsy cabs (unlicensed taxis) in upper Manhattan.

To buy a *bodega* costs a Dominican American about $150,000 to $200,000. The work involved in keeping the store profitable is very hard. The owners work 15-hour days and most weekends. They have to keep the prices low, so they often don't hire any help outside their families. The products they sell to their mostly Latino customers are foods familiar to them, such as plantains and the rice and beans that are staples of the Dominican diet. They also sell many groceries imported from the Dominican Republic.

The Dominicans soon also began buying businesses other than *bodegas* (also called *colmados*) and cab companies. Dominican Americans now own boutiques, jewelry stores, electronics stores—shops that cater to local and visiting Dominicans who

want to take gifts back to relatives in the Dominican Republic.
They also own hair salons (*peluquerías*) that cater to Dominican
customers, music shops that carry the latest merengue sounds,
and travel agencies that arrange trips back to the Dominican
Republic.

They have bought and refurbished restaurants all over the
New York City area as well as in Miami and other cities, creating a
new style of eatery. The Dominican restaurants or lunch counters,
called *fondas,* are structured like diners (with counters), but the
tables are nicely decorated with fresh flowers and tablecloths. The
food is labeled "Spanish and American" so that the appeal will be
universal. Once small "rice and bean joints," the restaurants are
now shiny new establishments with modern decor and varied
menus. The owners are usually older Dominicans who started
working in the restaurant business as busboys or dishwashers and
then moved up to become key restauranteurs.

The Media

Reviews of those restaurants may be found in some of the
many Dominican American newspapers in New York. Ten Spanish-
language newspapers in New York provide Dominican Americans
with news of their native country. At least one cable television sta-
tion carries Dominican programming for part of the day, and many
of the full-time Spanish-language stations report news from the
Caribbean country.

It was the Dominican American newspapers that carried criti-
cism of the Balaguer and Blanco presidencies to Dominicans in the

United States. The papers keep immigrants informed of the changes in immigration laws and print articles about how to deal with the complicated immigration system in the United States, as well as run stories about the local Dominican American community. They also maintain cultural ties to the Dominican Republic by advertising travel agencies, reporting baseball scores, and printing recipes.

Dominican Food

The food that appears at Dominican-owned restaurants is a unique combination of American traditional fare and the exotic flavors of the Dominican Republic. Dominican cuisine is an interesting array of Caribbean spices, produce, meats, and seafood used in a combination of traditional Spanish and African recipes. In the United States, this cuisine is a new addition to the already diverse assortment of Hispanic foods available.

The flavor of Dominican food starts with garlic, onions, coriander, and oregano. Similar to Cuban food, the basics include rice and red beans. But Dominican cuisine has a distinct African flavor that distinguishes it from its more Spanish Cuban cousin. Its African origins are reflected in the use of more root vegetables and meats such as goat.

One dish that epitomizes this union of cultures has become as much a tradition in Washington Heights as it is in the Dominican Republic. *Sancocho* is a yellow-orange stew made with chicken, beef, goat, or pork—or all four—plus African yams and other root vegetables (called *viveres* in the Dominican Republic).

Served with white rice and slices of avocado, it is a Sunday after-noon ritual in Santo Domingo. Now that ritual is ingrained in New York Dominican life.

Other traditional foods that are easy to find in Washington Heights restaurants include *tostones* (fried plantains served with *mojito* sauce made of raw garlic, lime, and olive oil), *chicharrón de pollo* (chopped chicken with peppery Dominican seasonings), *moro* (white rice with black beans and tomato sauce), and breaded pan-fried steaks. To accompany these dishes, Dominicans might order their favorite refreshment made from malted and condensed milks.

Some of the more exotic dishes include *habichuelas* (white beans in a thick pumpkin sauce), *flan con queso* (a typical Dominican dessert that is a cross between a custard and a cheese-cake), *sopa de camarones* (a shrimp broth laced with coriander), and *chivo guisado* (goat stewed with tomatoes, green peppers, and spices).

The Merengue Beat

Piping from the speakers of the Dominican restaurants, and from numerous windows in Washington Heights, are the musical sounds of the island country. Merengue is the traditional music of the Dominican Republic. Derived from Spanish music paired with an African beat, merengue is a Dominican version of salsa music.

Merengue has been called the cornerstone of Dominican nationalism in the United States, especially in New York. Many

continued on page 105

Esperanza Herrarte
Hoping In the Right Direction

Esperanza Herrarte operates a restaurant in Miami with her two sisters.

My restaurant is called The Three Sisters. We have a lot of fun, my sisters and I, running this place. Don't get me wrong, we work very hard, too; but being with family makes it easier. We all worked for years for other restaurants, mainly Cuban, before we had the money to open one of our own. Immediately, The Three Sisters was successful. It was one of the first restaurants in Miami that served food from the Dominican Republic. One thing you can say about us, we know how to cook our food!

We are all legal in our family. It started with my father's brother, then my father, then my brother, then my sister and her family, then me and my family, and then my youngest sister. We just keep coming, it seems. It is good that we can get here through family. I have friends back in Santo Domingo who are waiting years now to come here. Day after day they wait at the embassy—they fill out forms, they get denied. I tell them it is hard here, too, but at least there is a chance to make things better. They need to keep trying.

Miami is good. It is a little hard being in a Spanish-speaking community but being in the minority. Sometimes I feel that the Cubans think we are not quite so good as they are. You know how people are. Especially with all that is happening in Haiti now, we kind of get lumped together. Not so much with white

Americans. They don't even seem to know that the Dominican Republic is on the same island as Haiti! Not to complain, because everyone comes to our restaurant. This is kind of a surprise. We thought we would get only Dominican Americans. But, no, we get everyone. I think we are getting to be—what do the young people say?—hip.

My husband runs a cleaning service here in Miami. He used to do the work himself. Now he just sends people out where they need to go. He tries to be fair to the workers, because he remembers how hard it was on him at first. It's true, some of his employees are not legal. But I cannot judge that. People are people, and they need to work to eat.

Our children are learning different kinds of work and have different ideas about what to be and do. We were limited when we came here by the language and our education; they are not. I have a niece who is studying to be a writer at Columbia University in New York City. Imagine, she is a writer of English. I would never have believed this possible. She admires a writer from Dominican Republic, Julia Alvarez, who wrote a book called "How the Garcia Girls Lost Their Accents." She wrote it in English, but I read it in Spanish. I think I would never have read this book back home. I guess we all change even more than we think. My kids are doing good, too, but they are too young to be in college yet. They are still what you call a handful. I love American expressions.

Can I just tell you how good the food is at our restaurant? We have *sancocho* (a wonderful stew), *pollo frito*, fried plantains, and to start your meal, fresh

banana juice. Oh, we have much more, but why bore you to death. Come visit.
You walk through the door and the smells and flowers make you feel like you are
in a different world. This is the world I wanted when I came to this country. My
name in English means "hope." The Three Sisters is my reward for hoping in the
right direction.

✳ ✳ ✳

community events are punctuated by the strains of merengue music. Merengue artists perform regularly in the neighborhoods where Dominican Americans live, and they are popular among other Latino groups as well, such as Cubans, Puerto Ricans, and Colombians. There is even an annual merengue celebration—the Dominican Day Parade—every August in New York City.

Merengue music is played in nightclubs that are scattered around the Dominican neighborhoods. In these clubs one can also hear the other music enjoyed by the Dominican American population, including Latin hip hop, house music, rap, and new wave. But all Dominican Americans will tell you that merengue is the music they have heard since their earliest childhood days and that it is the sound they most associate with their Dominican heritage.

The Great American Pastime

Another place where merengue can always be heard is on the baseball fields in the parks of Manhattan. There, Dominican Americans gather to play the game that they grew up playing in the Dominican Republic. Their love for baseball is carried with them to the United States.

Dominican American business owners sponsor Little League teams, and entire families turn out (when they can get off work) to watch their children or brothers and sisters play. Social clubs form around the people who come from the same hometown in the Dominican Republic, and each club has its own baseball team. During games, the Dominican American teams blast merengue

Former New York City Mayor David N. Dinkins waves the Dominican flag as he marches in the annual Dominican Day Parade in Manhattan.

music, reminiscent of the bands that play between innings in Santo Domingo. Players sometimes work as merengue disc jockeys at parties to earn the money that pays for their equipment.

Each night, fathers and sons in Washington Heights and Spanish Harlem can be seen playing catch with a baseball and a couple of gloves. There is even an old-timers' league for the middle-aged men who still love the game. Mothers urge their sons to become good ball players so they can get scholarships to college or maybe even be drafted for the major leagues.

Baseball is one thing that ties the Dominican American community together. But it is also the link Dominicans have to native-born Americans. Baseball is the "great American pastime," but it is also the game of the Dominican Republic. It is just one of the many joys Dominicans find in their new life in the United States.

For Further Reading

Alvarez, Julia. *How the Garcia Girls Lost their Accents.* Chapel Hill, N.C.: Algonquin Books, 1991.

Dawson, Mildred Leinweber. *Over Here It's Different.* New York: Macmillan Publishing Co., 1993.

Dwyer, Christopher. *The Dominican Americans.* New York: Chelsea House, 1991.

Ferguson, James. *Dominican Republic: Beyond the Lighthouse.* London: Latin American Bureau, 1992.

Grasmuck, Sherri, and Patricia R. Pessar. *Between Two Islands: Dominican International Migration.* Los Angeles: University of California Press, 1991.

Kessner, Thomas, and Betty Boyd Caroli. *Today's Immigrants, Their Stories.* New York: Oxford University Press, 1982.

Wiarda, Howard J., and Michael J. Kryzanek. *The Dominican Republic: A Caribbean Crucible.* Boulder, Colo.: Westview Press, 1982.

Index